Everything You Need to Know About

LEARNING
DISABILITIES

Reading can be challenging for young people with learning disabilities.

Everything You Need to Know About

LEARNING DISABILITIES

Mary Bowman-Kruhm, Ed.D.
Claudine G. Wirths, M.A., M.Ed.

THE ROSEN PUBLISHING GROUP, INC.
NEW YORK

Thanks to Lorie Schaefer and the teachers at Seeliger Elementary in Carson City, Nevada, and to Teri Stetson at the Montgomery County, Maryland, public schools for their ideas and input.

Very special thanks to Dr. Richard Mainzer, Assistant Executive Director, Professional Standards and Practice, Council for Exceptional Children, for his expertise and help.

Published in 1999 by The Rosen Publishing Group, Inc.
29 East 21st Street, New York, NY 10010

First Edition

Library of Congress Cataloging-in-Publication Data

Bowman-Kruhm, Mary.
    Everything you need to know about learning disabilities / Mary Bowman-Kruhm, Claudine G. Wirths.
      p. cm. — (Need to know library)
    Includes bibliographical references and index.
    Summary: Examines what learning disabilities are and how they are assessed, as well as providing advice for coping with them in school, while having a social life, and in a career.
    ISBN 0-8239-2956-6 (lib. bdg.)
    1. Learning disabilities—Juvenile literature. 2. Learning disabled children—Juvenile literature. [1. Learning disabilities.] I. Wirths, Claudine G. II. Title. III. Series.
    RJ496.L4B68 1999
    616.85'889—dc21   99-17084
                                                         CIP
                                                           AC

Contents

Introduction

*"**I** hate the kids in my school, and I hate school, too," said Ray. He slammed his books on the kitchen table.*

"Tell me about it," said his mom as she handed him a soda.

"It's the same old thing. Some of the kids call me names like 'Retard' or 'Stupid,' and my teacher says if I just tried harder I could learn. But I DO try. I just can't seem to read words and make sense out of them like the other kids do. I know I'm smart, but when it comes to reading, I just don't get it!"

Ray has a learning disability. "Learning disability," or LD for short, is a term that is most often used to describe someone who has great difficulty doing well in school, especially in the language arts. A person with a learning disability has this difficulty in spite of having average to above average intelligence and good teachers in the early grades when reading and writing were first taught.

If you have a learning disability, if you know someone with a learning disability, or if you just want to know more about the problem, this book is for you. This book will focus on identifying a learning disability. We will tell you about some of the challenges people with learning disabilities face every day. We will also talk about some of the possible causes of LD. We will discuss how a learning disability can affect a teen's life in and out of school, and what a teen can do to help himself or herself in school and in finding a career. Finally, you'll learn what assistance teachers and LD specialists can give and how family and friends can help.

Learning may be more difficult for you if you have a learning disability, but you can do things to make it easier.

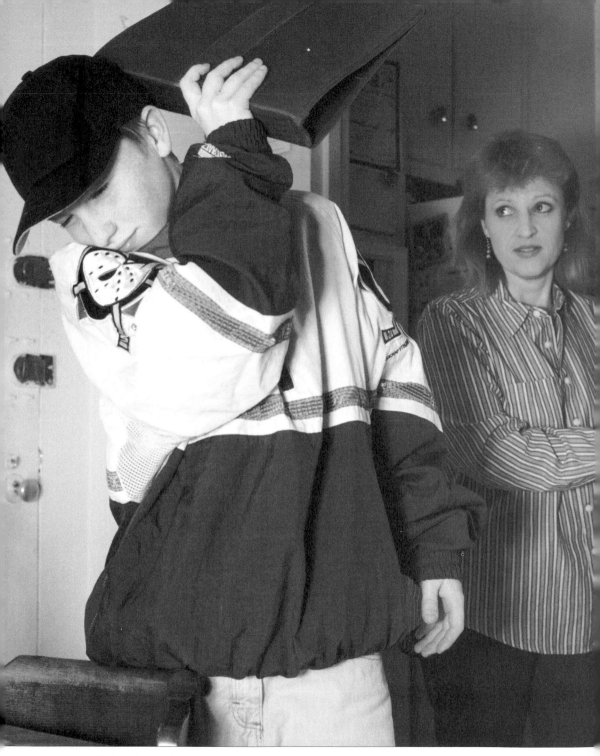
School can be very frustrating when you have a learning disability.

Chapter 1

What Is a Learning Disability?

Schoolwork is hard for many young people, and reading and writing can be hardest of all. However, some students have trouble linking what one part of their brain tells them with the information they get from another part of their brain. These students have average or above average intelligence, but—although they don't have vision or hearing problems—they have trouble making sense out of what they see and hear. The result of their difficulties is called a learning disability.

Trouble with Schoolwork

A learning disability often first shows up in school as a problem with learning to read, write, or do math. A learning disability may also cause someone to have speech and language problems; be poorly coordinated; not have a sense of space, distance, or direction; or have trouble organizing time, tasks, and belongings. Problems like these may in turn lead to social and emotional problems, such as anger, frustration, and difficulty getting along with others.

Ben has a learning disability. Even though he was a smart little boy, in first grade he had trouble learning to read. Now in ninth grade, he still does not read well. What he writes is hard to read, with lots of words spelled wrong. Math seldom makes sense to him. His desk and backpack seem ready to explode with a mess of papers, pencils, and odd things he throws in and forgets to take out.

"Try harder, Ben," his parents beg again and again. Ben grits his teeth. "I hate school," he says.

Learning Disability Doesn't Mean Lazy

Many people, even teachers, feel that a student who doesn't do well in school is lazy. "He (or she) seems smart. If only he would try harder," they say. The truth is that a person with a learning disability may not be lazy at all. He may try very hard to do well in school.

Suppose you play baseball or softball. Let's say you are very good at fielding but have trouble hitting because your timing is off. No matter what you do, your swing is either too quick or a split second behind. You want to be a really great player, so you work hard at your hitting. Your coach tries to help. You are at the field every spare minute because you want to be as good at hitting as you are at fielding. No matter how many hours you work on batting, are you sure to get hits? You may . . . or you may not.

A learning disability is much the same. If you have good teachers and work hard, you may do well in school . . . or you may not. If you don't, it doesn't mean that you're lazy.

A New Term for an Old Problem

In the 1920s in the United States, many teachers and parents noted that some children, in spite of average or above average intelligence, could not learn to read and write. One scientist gave the problem an interesting, if complicated, name. He called it strephosymbolia!

Naming the problem did not solve it, but it did get more people talking about it and searching for a way to help those who had trouble reading and writing. People began to use the more easily understood term "learning disability," or LD. Finally parents and teachers turned to the federal government and asked for help.

As a result, Congress passed Public Law 94–142 in 1975. This law said that all children with disabilities had the right to public education. Public Law 94–142 first defined the term "learning disabled," and the law has been amended, or added to, several times. It is now known as the Individuals with Disabilities Education Act, or IDEA.

Since 1975, as the term "learning disability" has come into use by educators and parents around the world, its meaning has broadened. This term has come to include a group of conditions that cause serious problems in listening, speaking, reading, writing, math, and reasoning.

Are These Learning Disabilities, Too?

You may hear other terms used to refer to problems with reading, writing, or doing math. These terms are similar to, but not quite the same as, "learning disability." To a specialist who works in this field or a special education teacher, each of these terms has its own precise meaning and characteristics.

Here are a few of these terms and their meanings:

- **Attention Deficit Disorder (ADD).** A student has difficulty paying attention and focusing on a task.
- **Attention Deficit Hyperactivity Disorder (ADHD).** A student has difficulty paying attention and staying focused and is overly active; a student with ADHD often does not think of the results of his or her actions before acting.
- **Dyslexia.** A student has severe problems with reading and writing. This term may include word blindness, in which a student cannot read words although she is able to tell the difference between individual letters. It also may include dysgraphia, in which a student has severe problems with handwriting, and dyscalculia, in which a student has severe problems with math.

- **Nonverbal Learning Disorders (NLD).** A student has excellent skills with language, but poor skills in the areas of motor, space, organization, and perception; he or she often has poor social skills, as well.

There are many more such terms. Because ADD and ADHD are so often associated with LD and may even be confused with LD, let's talk about them.

How Is LD Different from ADD and ADHD?

Students with ADD or ADHD are almost sure to also have a problem learning. If there is a dog barking outside or someone in the next seat is bumping her heels against a chair, a student with ADD is distracted from the test questions the teacher is writing on the board. He has trouble paying attention.

The student with ADHD may be the one bumping her heels. She may soon be bouncing off to the pencil sharpener in the middle of the test. Students with ADHD have a very hard time sitting still for even a few minutes. They seem compelled to move about. Because of their ADD or ADHD, these students may have difficulty learning and may do poorly in school. Even though students with ADD or ADHD have a problem learning, they may or may not have a learning disability.

The problems of ADD and ADHD must be treated apart from any learning disability. Often some form of

A learning disability sometimes makes it hard to concentrate.

medication can be helpful. A medication is any drug, prescribed by a doctor or sold over-the-counter, to help make someone feel better, do better, or get better. Camille's story is typical of someone who is not learning disabled but needs treatment for a mild form of ADD.

Camille was placed in honors classes when she began high school, but she didn't do very well. She complained that she found it very hard to pay attention and that she missed many things her teachers said. She had trouble focusing, especially in her afternoon classes.

Camille's language arts teacher wondered if Ritalin, a medication that helps many students with ADD pay better attention in school, might help. Her mother, school guidance counselor, and doctor discussed it, but they were not sure that Camille needed Ritalin.

"Please," Camille asked, "let me take it for a while to see if it helps." For a year Camille took two pills a day of the smallest amount of Ritalin possible. Soon she could stay focused on her schoolwork, and her grades improved.

Even though ADD and ADHD are not the same as LD, some specialists consider them a form of learning disability. About 20 percent of students who clearly are LD show some form of ADD or ADHD.

Does all of this sound confusing to you? If so, you are not the only one confused by all of these terms.

Dealing with LD can be confusing.

There are many issues that cause heated debate among doctors, teachers, specialists, and parents. These include what a learning disability is, what causes it, and how to identify and treat it.

What Causes LD?

Research to date shows no single cause for a learning disability. Learning disabilities often seem to be caused by a neurological problem, a problem the person has in his or her nervous system. Often a person is born with the learning disability.

This learning disability exists in spite of any other major problems a person has. Major problems can include emotional disturbance, when the person has one or more disorders of emotion, such as unfounded fears (phobias) or great sadness (depression). Major problems also include developmental delay (mental retardation). The person with developmental delay does not appear as intelligent as the average person. The delay can range from mildly retarded to severely retarded and is a lifelong problem. Other major problems might include deafness, a poor home life, and so on.

Some LD is inherited, meaning that it has a genetic cause. Genetic causes are conditions caused by the genes of the child's biological father and mother and are passed on to the child. Perhaps some LD results from different "brain wiring." A less common cause of LD is an accident at birth or later in life. It's hard to know for sure what exactly causes LD. Scientists are still working to find out what causes LD, and more important, how to prevent it.

Chapter 2

Who Has a Learning Disability?

*W*arren is captain of the football team and one of the most popular guys in his high school. With his curly blond hair and big blue eyes, he looks like a TV star on the local sports channel. Some people think he is the best player his high school has ever had. Hoping he will pick their college when he graduates, college football scouts hang around after every game to talk to him.

What the scouts don't know is that because of a learning disability, Warren will be lucky to graduate. He's barely passing his classes and even has a tough time learning the football plays. Every day after practice he takes the coach's plays and notes home to read and study with his dad. Warren works hard, but his learning disability was not recognized until he was in the eighth grade. He has a lot of catching up to do.

An Invisible Disability

Sometimes a bright, hardworking person like Warren fools teachers and parents for years before they notice serious learning difficulties. Because you can't see a learning disability, it is sometimes called an "invisible disability."

More often, now that parents and teachers are aware of learning disabilities, they suspect the problem early. To a parent, the child seems somehow different in the way he or she thinks and learns.

In school, the teacher soon notices that the child seems unable to put what is taught into practice. Not being able to sound out letters is one clue. Still another is not being able to hear words that have some of the same sounds. Another is not being able to pick out his or her name from a list of classmates' names. Such clues add up. Good teachers notice that a child is not learning along with the other students. By second and third grade, the problem becomes more obvious—the child doesn't keep up with classmates in reading, writing, and often math.

Do I Have a Learning Disability?

In everything we do, we range from "Wow!" to "Ugh!" Like the baseball or softball player who is a good fielder, each of us has things at which we are very good. These are our strengths, our "Wows!"

Also like the ballplayer, we have things we cannot do very well, no matter how hard we try. These are our weaknesses or problem areas. They are our "Ughs!"

Most often the "Ughs!" don't add up to a learning disability. Occasionally they do.

Right now you may be asking, "Do I have a learning disability?" Or you may be wondering if the problems a friend or sibling has mean that the person has LD. You may even wonder if a parent has a learning disability. Yes, even many older people go through life without understanding their learning problem. Recognizing LD is the first step in getting help for it.

The chart on the next page will help you decide if you or someone you know may have a learning disability.

Identifying LD

Identifying a learning disability is much harder than identifying many other problems. Even if you have lots of checks on the right side of the chart, you cannot be sure that you have a learning disability, although you would be wise to check it out.

Suppose you go to a doctor because you have a sore throat. The doctor sees that your throat is red and does a test to find the cause. If the test says that you have strep throat, then the doctor knows what the problem is and gives you the right medicine.

Unfortunately, no quick test yet exists that will allow a doctor or teacher to check numbers on a chart and then say for sure, "Yes, that person has LD." Correctly identifying LD is a long process that involves many people—the person with the problem, parents, doctors, teachers, and specialists. These people combine their findings to

Make a copy of this page to use as a worksheet. **DO NOT write on the page itself.**

Put a dot on the graph at the place that shows how you feel about your ability to carry out the activities listed. When you have put a dot for every item, look at where the dots fall.

- If most of your dots are on the right side of the graph, assessment by trained LD specialists is probably needed.
- If most of your dots are on the left side of the graph, you probably do not have a learning disability. You may, of course, still need help with reading, social skills, math, or any of the other areas in which you don't feel that you are at least "OK."

	Good Most of Time	OK Most of Time	Poor Most of Time
Coordination			
Reading ability			
Math ability			.
Ability to think before acting			
Ability to follow complex directions			
Attention span			
Memory for letters			
Memory for words			
Ability to tell right from left, north/south, east/west			
Handwriting			
Skill at organizing			
Sense of time			

decide if someone has a learning disability or if there are other causes for the problem. At times they find a complex mixture of many issues.

The first step in diagnosing, or discovering, a learning disability is calling on a group of specialists. Each specialist assesses the person in a variety of ways.

Assessment

The word "assessment" means "testing" or "evaluation." If your doctor wants to assess if you are overweight, she will measure your height and weight, compare the two, look at your bone structure, and measure the amount of your weight that is body fat. Then she can assess whether or not she thinks you are overweight.

Assessment for LD is also done by giving a series of tests and comparing the results. Some of the tests are formal ones in which questions are read and the answers given are recorded in a standardized way. Your results are compared against the results of many others who have taken that test.

Other tests are casual, informal assessments. A specialist watches and makes notes about how you do certain tasks. One task might be to read a story and answer questions about it. Notes made would include how long you took to read the story, what answers you gave to questions asked, and if you could find the correct answers to the questions you missed during a second reading.

Some of the areas commonly assessed include intelligence/thinking, reading, hearing, vision, math,

Testing someone for a possible learning disability is not easy.

writing, coordination and physical skills, social skills, and career skills (for older students).

Accurate Assessment Matters

Tests are hard and take a long time. An accurate assessment requires you to try your best with some-times boring, frustrating, and personal questions.

Before the doctor checks your weight, you would not fill the pockets of your jeans with lead weights. Likewise, if you are being tested for LD, you must not "load" the test answers, or answer dishonestly, to avoid being diagnosed as "different." If you don't cooperate fully, you only add to your problem and delay getting the help you may need.

23

What Does the Assessment Say?

Making the final diagnosis of LD is not simple. Sometimes it is clear that the person being assessed has a learning disability. All the tests and measurements and observations add up to say so. More often, though, the assessment results are not clear; other problems cloud the results.

For the school system to diagnose a student with a learning disability, the assessment must show that (1) the student is not sufficiently achieving for his or her age and level of ability; and (2) the primary reason for lack of school success is the learning disability rather than other possible causes.

Problems Often Confused with LD

Earlier we mentioned that some people who have ADD or ADHD have problems learning but that not all of them have a learning disability. Other conditions can cause you to appear to have LD when a different problem is the basic, or primary, trouble. These conditions include:

Physical problems of any kind, including problems with hearing and vision. Do you have a problem that can be treated, and if so, will the learning problem go away or at least be lessened?

Emotional problems. Are you feeling sad or angry or behaving in some way that is not acceptable?

Family, school, and social problems. You may have a problem learning because of family and personal conditions. Do you have a problem learning or a true learning disability?

Emotional problems caused by a parent's drinking can be mistaken for LD.

Sorting out a learning disability from any of the above is not easy. The last problem is one of the hardest to define. It includes all sorts of personal and family problems including alcoholism, abuse, illness, neglect, and many others. It also includes poor teaching, or at least teaching that did not match the way a child learns best.

Carlos has difficulty learning but is not learning disabled. He has a problem learning because of his family's lifestyle and the way he has dealt with it.

Carlos's family constantly moved from place to place when he was little. The family didn't have many belongings and owned very few books. Heavy books added to the cost of moving, and no one read much anyway. During first through fifth grades, Carlos attended nine different schools. Although his family wanted Carlos to learn and always enrolled him in school as soon as they found a place to live, he missed so many days that he did not learn to read very well. Finally he became so frustrated that he gave up and quit trying to read.

Finally, in the ninth grade, a sympathetic teacher realized why Carlos was having such problems reading. She talked him into working with her after school. With extra help Carlos soon began to learn to read and write better.

Although Carlos had serious problems with reading, he did not have a learning disability. His learning difficulties were caused by a family problem—constantly moving. However, unlike Carlos, many young people with similar problems are assessed and show a learning disability. Let's talk about how they can succeed.

Chapter 3

After the Assessment

Rafael, Sam, and Kris are in the tenth grade. Assessments for LD show that all three need help with reading and writing.

Rafael reads at a sixth-grade level. He understands most of what he reads, but he has trouble reading big words with lots of syllables. He likes to write on a computer, and with the help of a spell-checker, his teacher reports that he does well.

Sam reads at a fourth-grade level. He can pronounce most of the words but has trouble understanding complex ideas. His writing shows progress, but he has a lot of trouble reading his textbooks.

Kris reads at a second-grade level. Her reading ability is so poor that she has trouble understanding very easy stories. Her writing makes little sense even to her when she looks back on it a few days later. She is so upset by her school problems that she stays home from school whenever she can.

Help!

Several types of help are available if your assessment identifies you as having a learning disability. The help you receive depends on the results of the assessment.

Once you have been assessed, and before you are placed in a program, the law requires that you—and every child who is identified as needing special education services—have an Individualized Educational Program, better known as an IEP. This IEP must spell out your learning strengths and weaknesses, the special services you need, your special goals and objectives, a time line for checking on your progress, and the people assigned to carry out your program. In addition, the IEP must say how you will be part of the general education program.

This IEP must be reviewed and revised or rewritten every year in an annual review. You and your parents are invited to the meeting at which the team writes the IEP.

Although your parents can ask for a certain kind of help for you, they cannot ask for the use of special materials by name. They can, for example, point out that you need help with phonics. However, they cannot require a brand of phonics program in your IEP. How phonics is taught to you is up to the trained staff in your school.

Program Placement

You, your parents, and the school team must decide where the IEP will be carried out.

For a student with a mild learning disability, like Rafael, only a little extra help in his home or school may be needed. This student may spend a small part of the day getting extra help. He may get help within a regular classroom from an extra teacher or aide. This is called inclusion because the student with special needs is "included" in the general education classroom.

For a moderate disability, a student like Sam may spend part of the day in a class with small groups of students with special learning needs. This student could also get special help in an inclusion class.

A student like Kris, with a severe disability, may move to a private school or a special program in a public school. Kris would be part of a self-contained class. A self-contained class is a special classroom, usually within a school building, where students with special needs spend most of the school day. There, a trained staff structures every part of the day to meet each student's individual needs.

Feelings Matter in Program Choice

Both you and your parents, along with the school team, have input into the kind of program you receive. Part of the input you can have is to tell the team how you feel about being in special education.

Most students with LD have long known they were

different in some way. Putting a name to the problem may bring you a sense of relief, but students differ in their attitudes toward getting help. You may welcome classes with teachers who can help you deal with your disability. Or you may not want to be singled out. You may prefer inclusion in a regular class. For inclusion to succeed, you must be willing to try to learn. In successful inclusion programs, everyone benefits.

When the school and parents of a child with special needs do not agree on what should be done for the child, a person is called in to mediate—to look at both sides and help decide on what will be done.

Special Services

Often an assessment shows that a student needs special services outside of the general education classroom. Special services are services, other than school-based educational ones, needed by a person who has been assessed as having a learning disability. Some students may need to work with a speech and language therapist. Others need psychological counseling. Still others may need the services of a reading teacher. If any special services are needed, the school must provide the service.

What About a Tutor?

Students who have a learning disability often benefit from having a tutor at home. A tutor is a person who gives a student one-on-one help to learn a subject such as math.

Students with LD need to talk to their teachers about what works best for them.

One of the maddening aspects of a learning disability is that many students need constant help in overcoming the little gaps that make it hard to learn the whole of a concept. Suppose a student has her greatest problems in math. She learns to add and subtract but runs into problems grasping the steps of long division. An after-school math tutor can keep this student from falling too far behind.

A tutor should be trained to work with a learning disability. If the tutor is not specially trained, the student will be no better off. A student could even be worse off because her self-esteem as a learner will be hurt even more. Parents should ask the tutor if he or she holds a certificate or license as a special educator.

Home Schooling

Some parents, especially if they have LD themselves, know a lot about how children with LD learn. If their child is learning disabled, they may keep their child out of school for the first few grades and teach the child at home. They want to be sure that their child learns to read and is not teased by other children for being slow to learn.

One drawback to home schooling can be lack of contact with peers. For a student with LD who has problems socially, the transition from home schooling may be very hard. An active social life is important for all children and teens, but those with a learning disability may have more trouble than most finding and keeping friends. You can see chapter five, Friends and Feelings, for more information about these subjects.

Students who are home schooled may also not learn organizational skills. They do not learn to deal with such things as negotiating a large lunchroom, opening a locker, or changing into gym clothes. Although there are drawbacks to home schooling, there are advantages as well. Teachers, parents, and experts on education often debate the value of home schooling. However, almost all agree that if a student is home schooled, the transition from home schooling to organized education must be made very carefully. This is especially true if the student has a learning disability.

Home schooling in the early grades can be helpful to students with LD.

Gifted and LD

If you are a gifted student with a learning disability, you face special problems. In a gifted and talented class, you may not keep the pace needed in reading and writing. If left in regular classes, or even worse, if placed in special education classes, you may be bored. Your giftedness cannot be ignored in the IEP process. Like all other gifted young people, you need to be challenged regardless of your learning disability.

When the System Fails

When Towanda fell further and further behind in elementary and middle school, Towanda's mom asked for help. Somehow she didn't get it. By the end of tenth grade, everyone could see that Towanda would have to be held back—for the second time. Towanda's mother was worried that her daughter might never graduate from high school.

Her mother located Mr. Brown, a lawyer, who spoke with the school system staff about Towanda's needs. Mr. Brown pointed out how the federal law applied in Towanda's case, and the possible legal problems that might result if the school system did not help Towanda.

With Mr. Brown's help, Towanda was soon assessed for LD. When the assessment showed that she indeed had a learning disability, Towanda was given special services and tutoring to help her catch up.

Every community has resources to help people like Towanda and her mother. These resources are people called advocates. Advocate comes from a Latin word that means "to call." In this case, advocates call for the help students need for school success. It is not an easy job. Facing school staff and insisting that a student be placed in the right program and given the needed help takes time and hard work. A good advocate must also be outspoken and care about the person he or she represents. The advocate must also give a parent advice on what the parent can do, and help the parent to understand what the school system can and must provide, based on the law.

Some parents choose to hire lawyers who specialize in representing young people with learning needs. Of course, a lawyer will charge for his or her services. Other parents turn to churches, organizations, support groups, and state agencies that are willing to be advocates for students like Towanda for little or no cost. Such groups are often willing to give parents advice even if no one in the group actually speaks for them.

Today, parents can also find help and advice on-line. They are finding out that computers can link students, parents, and LD experts for the benefit of all. Some useful sources are listed in the Where to Go for Help section at the back of this book. Help is out there for parents and young people who face the problem of learning disabilities, especially for those who face a school system that seems unable or unwilling to provide the services needed.

Chapter 4

Coping at School

*T*o pass history tests, Dora knew that she needed to take lots of notes. She wrote much too slowly to be able to take down everything the teacher said. Often, while jotting down one fact or date or idea, she missed several more. Finally Dora asked the teacher if she could use a tape recorder. To Dora's surprise, her teacher answered, "Of course." Soon Dora had notes on tape that she could listen to over and over.

Like Dora, many people with a learning disability find that doing certain things a little differently from the way most people do them works well. They use areas of strength to compensate, or make up for, areas of weakness. They find tips and tricks that work.

Tips and Tricks That Work

We call our ideas tips and tricks, but the word educators use is "accommodations." Accommodations allow students with learning disabilities to get around, or to accommodate, problems by building on their strengths.

Think of accommodations this way: If you want to enter a door that is locked, you can bang and bang on the door and hope that it will pop open sooner or later. Or you can try to find a key to open it. For students with LD, trying to find the right key makes the most sense.

There are three types of accommodations. These deal with how information is presented and tested, what materials are used, and how the class is grouped. Many of the accommodations use technology such as computers and tape recorders, which helps the student make up for the lack of some skill or ability.

Many of the accommodations below can be used by all students, not only those with learning disabilities. Whether you have a mild or severe learning disability or have no trouble in school, you may find some ideas that will help you learn better and more easily. Note: The school may allow a student with an IEP to use only some of them, like dictating a test into a tape recorder. Get permission from your teacher before you try these strategies in class.

How Information Is Presented and Tested

Students with a learning disability usually do better:

- In classes with teachers who provide high structure and give clear directions about what they
  expect the student to do.
- In classes where teachers use short sentences and
  a simpler vocabulary, speak more slowly, and
  repeat important facts.
- If they take notes on what the teacher says. Some
  teachers will also allow extra help, such as using
  a tape recorder for note-taking, copies of notes
  from a student who takes good notes, or copies of
  the teacher's notes.
- If they use a tape recorder or computer for class
  assignments, including test-taking.
- If they are given special test-taking accommodations, such as taking an untimed test, testing
  orally, dictating answers to a person or a tape
  recorder, or taking the test on a computer.
- If they are allowed to use taped books for some
  classes. The Library of Congress provides a special tape recorder and taped books. Many schools
  and libraries also have a variety of books on tape.

What Materials Are Used

Students with a learning disability usually do better:

- If they get organized. Each student needs to find his
  or her best way to organize time, schoolwork, and
  personal stuff. A student may need help in finding a
  way to organize that works best for him or her.

Tape recorders can be a big help when taking notes in class.

- If they keep a calendar. They don't rely on memory if remembering is hard for them.
- If they use a homework sheet with space for tomorrow's assignments and long-term projects.
- If they use some trick to remember books and materials that will be needed. One example is jotting down the books and materials needed for homework on a note on the homework sheet.
- If they find books that cover the same concepts but are easier to read. If the teacher cannot help find those materials, the school librarian or the children's librarian at the public library can.
- If they try to find other media that present the information needed. These include filmstrips, videos, movies, and audio tapes.
- If they draw pictures and make notes to aid memory. For example, when studying colonial times, draw a log cabin and write important dates on each log.
- If they use concrete materials, such as pie-shaped pieces for learning fractions or raised letters for learning the alphabet and numbers.

How the Class Is Grouped

Students with a learning disability usually do better:

- If they ask the teacher if they can buddy up with someone. For example, a report on World War II may require interviewing and writing a paper about someone who was in the war. If the student with LD is good at setting up a tape recorder and asking questions, he or she can volunteer to do the interview. The buddy can write the report and print it out.

- If they don't pick friends as their buddies but choose people who have strengths in areas different from theirs.
- If they don't just ride along on their buddy's work but do their share of the work.
- If they tell the teacher they want to work alone, if that's how they work best.

General Problems at School

Most students with LD have problems with academic subjects. However, those same problems of reading, sequencing (putting information in the proper order, such as the letters of the alphabet or days of the week), timing, and social clumsiness carry over to many aspects of school life.

A student who does not sequence easily may have trouble finding the right locker in a long row of numbered lockers. Remembering the locker combination is an even bigger problem. If the student has problems with timing as well, he may continue to fiddle with the lock and try to crack the code. Result? Late for class.

Some students don't have to deal with the hassle of a locker but are still late to class. If a student has timing problems she may get so involved in talking with

LD can cause trouble with remembering locker combinations.

a friend that she misjudges the time she needs to walk to a class at the far end of the building. She also may not finish her lunch quickly enough so that she has time to go to the restroom before her next class starts.

Since many students with LD tend to count on a regular schedule to help them know where to go and what to do next, snow days with shortened schedules or special assemblies that drop the last class may be extremely confusing. The student may go to the wrong class or fail to show up at all.

Some students find that they survive school better if they develop a friendship with a buddy. Together they can play off one another's strengths to handle the cafeteria line or read school notices.

Having a learning disability is a real difficulty all day long for the person who suffers from it. At the final class buzzer, most students with a learning disability are utterly worn out from the sheer effort they have put out just to live through a school day.

Thomas, a senior, pulled his favorite teacher into a corner of the cafeteria where no one could hear them.

"Quick, help me," he said as he thrust a piece of paper into her hand. "Write something short that I can copy and write in people's yearbooks. I don't know what to do when they hand me their books. Make it funny, too."

Many of the ideas previously listed put the responsibility on you—the student—for taking action or asking for help from others. Each of us is our own best teacher. Taking charge of one's learning is good for everyone, including those with learning disabilities.

If you have a learning disability, you should not expect easy answers or any one way to solve all of your school problems. No one program will quickly teach you to read; no one tip will make your life easy; no one piece of equipment holds the key to getting As. Even so, many people with learning disabilities succeed, and you can be one of them.

Chapter 5

Friends and Feelings

No matter how hard he tried, Frank couldn't seem to make friends. He went out of his way to ask other guys at school about a test or sports, but they soon moved away when he started talking to them.

"What am I doing wrong?" he asked his counselor.

"I was watching you the other day, Frank, and I think you are having a hard time knowing when to talk and when to keep quiet," his counselor replied. "A conversation is like jumping rope. You have to know when and how to jump in. You also have to know when to stand back and listen. I saw you go up to a group of guys who were talking about the school dance. Instead of waiting for Shawn to finish what he was saying, you jumped in and asked Jack a loud question about his basketball game."

"Well, you said that if I wanted to make friends, I

had to ask people about things that interest them, and I know Jack likes basketball."

"You had the right idea, but you picked the wrong time and the wrong way and the wrong place to ask the question."

Frank shook his head. "I guess I see what you mean, but . . ." His voice trailed off. "But I don't, really."

Getting Along with Others

As we grow up, we learn how to get along with others. For example, most of us learn at an early age to read body language. When people use body language, they use their bodies to communicate their feelings in ways such as smiling, frowning, and standing with their arms crossed. When someone pulls back from us, we understand we are too close to him or her. A yawn tells us that someone may be bored.

Many people with a learning disability, like Frank, are often not good at reading the body language of other people. For lots of reasons, they don't seem able to notice subtle signals such as a lifted eyebrow or a frown.

Like Frank, some people with LD may also have a poor sense of timing. They can't judge when to bring a new topic into a conversation or how to get to a party on time.

There is almost no end to the ways a learning disability can interfere with one's social life. Here are some other examples.

Shyla skips too many spaces when she plays a board game. She doesn't "see" the correct number of spaces. Friends think she is cheating.

Brandon may quit listening to someone because he is still trying to make sense of the first words he heard. People think he's not paying attention to them.

Devon has problems remembering. One day he could not remember where his mom hid the house key. He was so frustrated that he kicked a hole in the door. Devon's parents grounded him for a month.

Frustration Is Frustrating

One of the most common results of social problems for the person with LD is frustration. Frustration is a deep sense of distress at not being able to solve a problem or not getting something you need. Because most people with LD have average or above average intelligence, their minds tell them that they should be able to play a board game or find a key. They may be frustrated when they don't succeed. When someone is frustrated, what is the person likely to do? Frustration usually leads to anger.

When angry, some people turn the anger inward. They blame themselves and become depressed. This is the loner in the cafeteria who turns down offers to eat with others. This is the girl who stays in class during assemblies and pep rallies to do homework. This is the boy who never talks to anyone.

The frustration of dealing with LD can make people angry at their friends.

Other people, when angry, blame everyone else. This is the kid who yells at her teacher for a bad grade or hits someone after he stumbles over his own foot. Sometimes such kids become known as troublemakers. It's hard for them to keep friends because they're always angry.

Why So Serious?

Why is the problem of frustration so serious? Think about these facts. About 40 percent of students with LD drop out of school. Thirty to 50 percent of American youth and adults convicted of crimes have learning disabilities. About 40 percent of teenagers who commit suicide in the United States and Canada were previously assessed as having a learning disability.

The constant frustration of not achieving as much as others wears down emotional resources. Since the disability is invisible, it is often overlooked because the person denies the disability or fails to let others know about it. The person worries in silence rather than asking for or accepting support. Help shrinks; frustration grows.

Other people with LD learn to laugh at themselves as a way of handling frustration. They turn their feelings into humor. A number of successful comics have a history of learning disability and are remembered by classmates as "class clowns." Classmates like to be around someone who makes them laugh—but class clowns are not always popular with teachers.

Other young people blame themselves and become profoundly depressed. Depression is a serious state of sadness that gets in the way of working or studying or living well. Tragically, this severe frustration may end in a suicide attempt. Sooner or later, almost all young people with LDs seek to avoid the pain and frustration of their disability. Too often they use alcohol or other drugs to numb their pain.

Today young people, along with the help of parents and teachers, are learning that counseling—and often medicine—can help them to cope with the frustration they feel and the ways in which they express this frustration.

School and Community Can Help

Good school programs can help a great deal. The best programs are based on current research and designed

Unfortunately, some kids deal with the stress of LD by using alcohol and drugs.

to meet the needs of a school's students. They are supervised by capable administrators and staffed with professionally trained, sensitive teachers and support staff. Such programs help students with LD make academic progress.

Good programs must also help students with LD fit comfortably into the school and make friends. Administrators should make sure all of the teachers—not just the special education staff—understand the special problems of students with learning disabilities. They should make it clear that teachers are not to call any students "dumb" or "lazy," nor make other remarks that are put-downs.

In turn, teachers should likewise be firm with students

who name-call. Most students do much better with positive comments about their successes and direct help with weaknesses.

Many schools or community groups, like the local learning disabilities parent group, provide training in social skills for students with LD. In schools, the counselors work both formally and informally with students.

Some of the social skills that counselors and group leaders work to correct include the following:

- Language—babyish words, constant cursing, stuttering
- Immature behavior—crying, teasing others, playing with toys meant for younger children, playing with younger children
- Poor sense of social timing—ignoring others, interrupting others, talking too long or too much
- Hostile behavior—blaming others, cruel teasing of classmates, fighting, theft, vandalism, stalking
- Self-defeating behavior—failure to join school clubs or athletics, staying alone, taking drugs or alcohol, going along with others just to fit in

Getting the right help is important because young people with LD grow up to be adults with LD. The choices you make during your school years directly impact your life after school.

Chapter 6

LD Lasts a Lifetime

Because of Tom, the camping trip was a night-mare for everyone in the family. What should have been fun turned into shouting and crying and unhappiness. Tom is not an angry teen—Tom is the dad, and he has a learning disability.

When the family tried to put up the tent, the poles had to be laid out in the same order every time. The tent had to be folded exactly the same way when it was put away the next morning. Tom's insistent pushing that things be done his way—and his getting angry when the family complained—ruined the fun.

A learning disability lasts for life. Although it is most often seen as a problem during the school years, the truth is that no one outgrows LD.

LD Affects Home Life

Home is where most people learn the basic tasks of living. Parents begin teaching children as soon as they are born. Of course, there are conflicts all through the learning process as children grow up, but since most of us are born eager to learn, learning usually happens rather easily.

The process can become very complex and riddled with problems if one of the family members has a learning disability. Not only is the learning process difficult, but the daily threads of family life may be strained to the breaking point.

Such a family soon learns that they must make adjustments. The person with a disability has to make adjustments, too. Using a disability as an excuse for not joining fully in the family and not carrying one's load of family jobs doesn't work and isn't fair.

Tom's son Hank also has a learning disability. Hank is eighteen, and he will soon graduate from high school. He's still not able to read well and has many of the problems that go along with LD.

Hank's room is a mess, and he can never find anything. He often arrives at school without his homework (when he remembers to do it) or money for lunch. He usually gives up on finding his keys before he leaves and decides he'll worry about getting in the house when he gets home. When his mother tells him to do something, he stands and looks at her blankly, so she has to repeat herself. She often mutters angrily, "You're just like your father!"

Hank's mother worries about what will become of him. What kind of job can he get?

What Happens After High School?

Older high school students and young adults with learning disabilities face serious career choices. Sadly, some students graduate unable to read or write at the level needed for a well-paying job. Others drop out before graduation. These teens are lacking the job skills and work habits needed for career success.

If you are determined to get an education or a diploma, you must work hard and want to achieve. Then, with wise, thoughtful choices, a career and/or college can be part of your future. You must find the right school and eventually the right career and learn how to build on your strengths and maneuver around your weaknesses.

Getting Career Help

Everyone has things they do best. If you have a learning disability, you must build on your strengths. If you tend to be creative, for example, you may make an excellent photographer or artist, or work onstage or off in drama productions. Whereas some people with LD have trouble getting along socially, others are "people persons" who excel in jobs where they deal with the public, as long as little reading and writing are required.

Celebrities with LD like Steven Spielberg have built upon strengths and worked around weaknesses to succeed.

Finding a career counselor is a good first step. This person can be a high school counselor or can be found through a public agency or private company. A career counselor can help you to get the career education that you need. A career education will teach you the skills you need to live on your own, cope with daily problems, and get a job.

To make the leap from a job to a lifetime career, you may need more training after high school. A counselor can help you find the right college or training program. Although all colleges must provide some accommodations for the learning disabled, a growing number specialize in helping and supporting those with LD. The counselor can also help you find a career area that builds on your strengths and gets around your weaknesses.

Because Hank liked to be outside, his counselor suggested that he apply for an opening as a lawn maintenance worker in a nearby state park. For the first time, Hank became excited about a job.

The counselor told him, "Hank, you say you really want this job. To keep it, you'll have to remember to take your tools, and whatever else you'll need for the day, to work. You'll also have to stay focused on the work you're doing and what the boss tells you to do. I'll talk to the boss about your problem understanding directions, but you have to listen and then repeat what you think he said. You can't just shrug and do your own thing."

Strengths and Weaknesses

Maneuvering around weaknesses is like making an end
run in football. It doesn't mean taking the easy way out;
it means getting where you want to go by taking a different path.

*Hank and his counselor talked about his problem
with organization. Together they made a checklist. As
Hank packed his lunch and got his clothes ready the
night before his first day, he checked those items off. He
agreed to take out the trash if his mom would make
sure he got out of bed when the alarm went off each
morning. "Take out trash" was added to his checklist.
As he left the house, he stopped at a small table by the
door for his keys and then checked off the last item,
"Pick up keys." The checklist helped Hank with his
problem with organization.*

What Kind of Career?

The key to a successful career is finding the right
resources—human or manufactured—in whatever field
a person chooses. If an adult with LD wants to go into
business, for example, he or she may need a partner to
handle some aspects of it.

*After several years of working at the park, Hank
wanted to start his own yard-service business. By now
he knew his strengths. Because he still loved outside
work, no matter what the weather, he was willing to work*

Developing one's strengths is the key to living successfully with a learning disability.

hard and put in the hours needed. He also knew he had weaknesses, and knowing how to run a business was one of them.

With the help of his family, he became partners with Rosa, a young woman with a business background. Rosa handled the paperwork, ordered supplies, and made hundreds of telephone calls. Together they worked out estimates for customers. Soon they had several other people working for them.

Help and Hope

Living with a learning disability is not easy. Neither is living with someone who has a learning disability.

Fortunately there are some excellent books and

materials that give practical advice to both teens with LD and their families. A number of on-line bulletin boards and Web pages can also provide information. You can find material on everything from ratings of reading programs to software for banking to kind words for soothing frustration. Some of these resources are listed in the back of the book in the section called Where to Go for Help.

Because there are so many differences in families and in each individual, suggestions that work in one situation or for one person may not work well in another. But you and your family should keep working and trying for a sense of harmony. Many people with LD have gone on to lead successful, productive, and fulfilling lives. It is possible, and you can do it.

Glossary

accommodations Things that a student needs to be successful; for example, untimed tests and audio-taped books.

advocate A person who helps parents and students get or improve the special services that must be provided by the school.

assessment Testing of a student to determine if there is a need for special education services.

compensate To use a strength to overcome a weakness, such as using a computer to write papers if a person has trouble with handwriting.

home schooling Schooling that takes place in the home, usually under the direction of a parent.

inclusion Educating a student with special needs in a general education classroom.

learning disability A disorder that causes a person of average or above average intelligence to have greater difficulty with reading, writing, math, listening, thinking, or talking.

self-contained class Special classroom, usually within a school building, where students with special needs spend most of their day.

special services Services other than educational ones needed by a person who has been assessed as having a learning disability.

Where to Go for Help

In the United States

AVKO Educational Research Foundation
3084 West Willard Road, Suite P
Clio, MI 48420-7801
(810) 686-9283
Web site: http://www.iser.com/AVKO.html
e-mail: DonMcCabe@aol.com

Will answer questions related to dyslexia and/or learning disabilities via telephone, fax, or e-mail. Provides tutoring and training for parents, teachers, and community volunteers. Publishes a variety of inexpensive materials for students with learning disabilities. Examples: *Sequential Spelling, Improving Spelling via Keyboarding,* and *The Proper Editing of Notes: The Key to Successful Learning.*

Council for Exceptional Children
1920 Association Drive
Reston, VA 20191
(888) CEC-SPED
Web site: http://www.cec.sped.org

An international professional association of special educators with an active program to improve learning for people with special needs. Many books and materials. Web pages updated weekly with current news about special education.

International Dyslexia Association
8600 LaSalle Road, Chester Building, Suite 382
Baltimore, MD 21286-2044
(800) ABCD-123
Web site: http://www.interdys.org

Offers information and resources on dyslexia.

Learning Disabilities Association (LDA)
4156 Library Road
Pittsburgh, PA 15234
(412) 341-1515
Web site: http://www.ldantl.org
e-mail: ldantl@usaor.net

Offers basic information on learning disabilities and has large numbers of books, pamphlets, and videos for sale and rent.

National Center for Learning Disabilities
381 Park Avenue South, Suite 1401
New York, NY 10016
(888) 575-7373
(212) 545-7510
Web site: http://www.ncld.org

Nonprofit organization provides resources and information on learning disabilities.

In Canada

Learning Disabilities Association of Canada (LDAC)
323 Chapel Street, #200
Ottawa, Ontario K1N 7Z2
(613) 238-5721
Web site: http://edu-ss10.educ.queensu.ca/~lda
e-mail: ldactaac@fox.nstn.ca

Nonprofit organization conducts programs and provides information in both English and French on learning disabilities.

For Further Reading

Beal, Eileen. *Everything You Need to Know About ADD/ADHD*. New York: Rosen Publishing Group, 1998.

Hall, David E. *Living with Learning Disabilities: A Guide for Students*. Minneapolis, MN: Lerner Publications, 1996.

Knox, Jean M. *Learning Disabilities*. New York: Chelsea House, 1989.

Lewis, Ann. *Children's Understanding of Disability*. New York: Routledge, 1995.

Wirths, Claudine G., and Mary Bowman-Kruhm. *I Hate School: How to Hang In and When to Drop Out*. New York: HarperCollins, 1992.

Videos

I'm Not Stupid (53 minutes, 1987). A discussion by students who are learning disabled. Purchase from Learning Disabilities Association (LDA), 4156 Library Road, Pittsburgh, PA, 15234. Tel: (412) 341-1515. Other videos and audiotapes available on various topics.

Index

About the Authors

Dr. Mary Bowman-Kruhm and Claudine G. Wirths have authored more than twenty books together. Their work ranges from a picture book (written under the pen name C. W. Bowie) to beginning readers for children and nonfiction for young adults.

Bowman-Kruhm is a senior faculty associate in the Department of Special Education, School of Continuing Studies, at Johns Hopkins University in Baltimore. She is a contributing editor to the newsletter *Children's Book Insider*. For twenty-five years, Bowman-Kruhm was a special education teacher and administrator for the Montgomery County, Maryland, public schools.

Wirths holds master's degrees in both psychology and special education. She retired from her position as coordinator of a program for students with learning disabilities to write full-time. Wirths enjoys mentoring adults and helping them discover the personal pleasures of writing.

Photo Credits

Cover Photo by Brian T. Silak.
P. 54 © Everett collection; p. 33 © Kevin Laubacher/FPG International; pp. 2, 57 © Skjold Photographs. All other photos by Brian T. Silak.